YOUR KNOWLEDGE HAS VALUE

Nick Birch

Surviving as a "Software as a Service" (SaaS) Startup

GRIN Publishing

Bibliographic information published by the German National Library:

The German National Library lists this publication in the National Bibliography; detailed bibliographic data are available on the Internet at http://dnb.dnb.de .

Imprint:

Copyright © 2015 GRIN Verlag GmbH
Print and binding: Books on Demand GmbH, Norderstedt Germany
ISBN: 978-3-656-88229-9

This book at GRIN:

http://www.grin.com/en/e-book/287995/surviving-as-a-software-as-a-service-saas-startup

GRIN - Your knowledge has value

Since its foundation in 1998, GRIN has specialized in publishing academic texts by students, college teachers and other academics as e-book and printed book. The website www.grin.com is an ideal platform for presenting term papers, final papers, scientific essays, dissertations and specialist books.

Visit us on the internet:

http://www.grin.com/

http://www.facebook.com/grincom

http://www.twitter.com/grin_com

Surviving as a SaaS Startup (SaaSaaSS)

Nick Birch 2015

SECTION 1: INTRODUCTION

Software as a Service (SaaS) is changing the way businesses operate. It's not just a trend: it's a proven way for small business owners to save time and money. We owe it all to the cloud for ushering SaaS into the business world.

When examining the basics of running a business, a single subscription to a SaaS app could take the place of an entire department. Small businesses and start ups can have email, file storage, expenses, purchasing, human resources, collaboration and task management at a lower cost for IT and software. With access to services and software that was once only available to huge companies because of the high cost of infrastructures and maintenance, software services allow a business to cut costs and focus on their product and services instead of setting up elaborate software or delegating between departments.

As a startup in the SaaS space, it is a long and perilous journey just to survive, let alone be notably successful. As the marketplaces have become quickly crowded, just finding a niche deems very difficult, let alone actively dominating one. The big players easily establish themselves, offering freemium cloud storage and software build upon already successfully proven programs. Microsoft now offers its Office suite in the cloud and Google has its slew of online business tools, all as various and competitively priced monthly subscriptions. Other startups moved in quickly at the outset, snatching up software real estate and thriving: Basecamp for project management, Freshbooks for accounting, Salesforce for customer relationship management, Pinterest for project and interest discovery, Snapchat for innovative mobile conversation, the list goes on (Vidra, 2014).

So what exactly does it take to survive as a SaaS startup in today's information age?

Technological innovation, design, strong business models and customer attraction and retention all seem to be at the forefront of SaaS culture, although the difference between short and long-term success may be more elusive than any particular set of recipes for permanence.

SECTION 2: RESEARCH QUESTION

By examining various contemporary business acumen of SaaS startups, contributing factors of a company's durability will hopefully emerge. This may be achieved by first discovering what experts believe to be at the heart of entrepreneurship, innovation, marketing and monetisation using several examples before pitching two similar companies side-by-side over the course of their lifespans to date.

'Entrepreneurs sacrifice sleepless nights and their life's savings in pursuit of building a product or a service that not only fills a need but changes people's lives. In the world of startups, we're all watching and waiting for the next big thing — for a company to come out of nowhere, do something amazing and make a ton of money; hopefully changing the world along the way' (Fell, 2014).

Zwilling (2013) notes that the 'problem is that professional investors (Angels and Venture Capital) want a proven business model before they invest, ready to scale, rather than the more risky research and development efforts'. In the meantime, many startups focus on their product and reaching their users — adopting bootstrapping or lean models, building a minimum viable product (MVP), validating it, procuring funding or sustainable revenue, and finally scaling (Maurya, 2010).

But first, users need to be not only acquired, but activated into revenue-producing customers. Assistant professor of marketing at Harvard Business School, Vineet Kumar (2014), says that 'over the past decade, "freemium"—a combination of "free" and "premium"—has become the dominant business model among startups and app developers. Users get basic features at no cost and can access richer functionality for a subscription fee. If you've networked on LinkedIn, shared files through Dropbox, watched TV shows through Hulu, or searched for a mate on Match, you've experienced the model firsthand'.

Is the problem of long-term success connected to the origins, purpose or mission of the business? Or whether it can "pivot" by changing direction to keep with the times and customer needs? Is its initial priority to acquire users or profits? And how do they manage the threats of the marketplace in the early stages?

It seems SaaS startups have many problems to face while getting up on their feet. By examining these areas and their potential solutions in greater detail, we may begin to understand more about what is essential, what is incidental and what potentially works in the longterm.

SECTION 3: LITERATURE REVIEW

Gompers and Lerner (2001) reveal that 'a growing body of research shows that individuals make decisions based on biased assessments of information. These assessments are powerfully influenced by people's beliefs about themselves and the workings of business. Most entrepreneurs are certain that their venture will succeed — despite the fact that nearly half of all venture capital-backed companies don't fulfil their potential and nearly one-third go out of business. For newly launched enterprises without venture capital backing, failure is almost assured: nearly 90 percent fail within three years'.

The following excerpt shows that historically, major business mistakes have ended fledging software companies since the beginnings of personal computer software development:

> In the early 1980s, Tom Gregory and a group of his colleagues from a minicomputer software company decided to enter the personal computer software market and compete head-to-head with Lotus and Microsoft. The company they founded, Ovation Technology, raised over $6 million in venture capital financing. Gregory and his founding team possessed extensive marketing backgrounds but scant technical skills. So, perhaps not surprisingly, Gregory's team decided to spend substantial resources on marketing — at the expense of research and product development.

> Out of the gate, Ovation began spreading the word about major improvements in functionality that their program would offer over their competitors. Its polished advertising campaign excited the imaginations of potential customers and investors, and gave them the impression that the company was thriving. Current investors, however, found it difficult to gauge the progress of the company. Although Ovation gave them glowing reports of the company's supposedly significant strides, they never presented a completed prototype. In fact, the company never finished developing its product — and never made a significant sale. If the founders had shared the necessary information with investors, perhaps Ovation's venture capitalists could have guided Gregory along the development path and this failure could have been averted.

> (Gompers and Lerner, 2001)

Gompers and Lerner (2001) are of the opinion that 'entrepreneurs will almost always choose to continue spending money to market their product or develop their technology — even when the evidence clearly shows that they should abandon their efforts. Similarly, overly optimistic entrepreneurs may feel compelled to expand their firm's capacity beyond its requirements because they overestimate the future demand for their products'. It's what Agrawal (2014) calls 'the difference between short-term capitalism and long-term capitalism. You have to optimise your strategy for the society we live in, not a theoretical perfect market'.

Evernote VS Springpad

With the ever-growing noise and mess of content on the Web and on social networks, people are increasingly looking for better ways to curate their digital experiences and channel that white noise into signal.

> *Springpad has long been considered a rival of the popular productivity app, Evernote, as both fundamentally seek to act as a memory aid for busy people, allowing users to capture anything and everything within apps or on the Web, and easily search content by keyword and tags. Yet, while Evernote has blown up in the past two years, soaring past 20 million users, Springpad has quietly been plugging along — adding features and building a viable competitor.*
>
> *(Empson, 2012)*

In a video from the Creative Industries Innovation Centre (see Appendix A), Digital Media Manager for Film Victoria, Brad Giblin, says: 'It's very, very crowded in these marketplaces today... [I]t's a lot more innovative in terms of the business models, the distribution platforms and also the audiences. So you can afford to look at mechanisms to raise financing off pledges, off Facebook drives, off your friends and family, off pre-sales... sell portions... packages... sell limited editions or special versions that enable you to have some kind of revenue in the production phase and hopefully then further revenue when you come to sell it down the track' (Creative Innovation, 2010).

Is this kind of impermanence commonplace? Do most startups begin with the intention to flip?

Evernote CEO, Phil Libin, gives a candid contradiction: 'It never starts out with how much money can we make. It never starts out with how many of these can we sell? It starts out with what's the point of it; why is the world better off because this product has existed in it? If the world isn't better off because the product existed in it then it's just not interesting to make' (Baer, 2013).

Libin isn't interested in flipping his cloud note-taking company. In fact, he says it has 'no exit strategy, despite the fact that it has amassed 80 million users and raised $US250 million' (Shontell, 2013). Instead, they want to create what they call a "100-year startup", consisting of two parts:

1. It should be a company that's around in 100 years, which means Evernote's product needs to be durable.

2. It should still be a startup in 100 years, which means it should still be an innovative company that people love (Shontell, 2013).

Founded in 2008, startup Springpad was designed as an organiser app for 'recipes, movies to watch, home improvement projects, and interior design projects' (Ungerleider, 2014). They focused more on the short-term marketplace, where their product fit and what differentiated them from the crowd. Springpad's former head of user engagement, Katin Miller, laments: 'We see so many apps coming out now doing what we were doing, but the market is so thirsty for it now. If we had come out a few years later and been mobile first, it may well have been a different ending' (Ungerleider, 2014). Springpad says that its growth had been fuelled by mobile adoption. Nearly half of its users were using its Android app and a third using Springpad via an iOS device (Rao, 2011).

Their core product was designed for clipping items for later purchase, 'but their 2008 launch date occurred before the mobile app economy fully bloomed' (Ungerleider, 2014). Miller believes that their user base was their strength: 'We had an evolved user-base we listened to and integrated into our needs and decision making. Springpad had a talented team, and when we talked to other tech companies... people were amazed by what we had done with less than 20 employees. We never had more than 20 people on staff at any one time, and had three polished and powerful apps on the market' (Ungerleider, 2014).

For a basic overview of startup metrics for internet marketing and product management, a simple model was devised in 2008. Dave McClure is the founding partner of 500 Startups, an internet startup seed fund and incubator in Silicon Valley with over $125M under management (500hats, N/A). He created 'an amazing deck in 2008 called "Startup Metrics for Pirates: AARRR" (details in Appendix B) and it's still incredibly relevant today' (Mullin, 2013). Essentially, McClure broke down the components of the startup analytics acronym into five categories:

A: Acquisition - where / what channels do users come from?

A: Activation - what % have a "happy" initial experience?

R: Retention - do they come back & re-visit over time?

R: Referral - do they like it enough to tell their friends?

R: Revenue - can you monetise any of this behaviour?

(Ford, 2012)

Acquisition

As an example of rapid acquisition, the formerly popular video sharing app, Viddy, was a viral app that grew rapidly by getting a user to sign up using their Facebook account and then sharing this action with their friends, social media always being a popular method of the third "R" - Referral.

In the first part of the "500 Distribution" series on activation for SaaS, content producer Susan Su (2014) thinks that '[m]ost SaaS companies are (rightly) concerned with user acquisition but fail to pay adequate attention to activation. What few realise is that activation plays a major role in user acquisition itself'.

This graph from the article "Retention is King" by Managing Partner of Quint Growth, Jamie Quint (N/A), shows 'what happens when you are crushing user acquisition but failing to activate users':

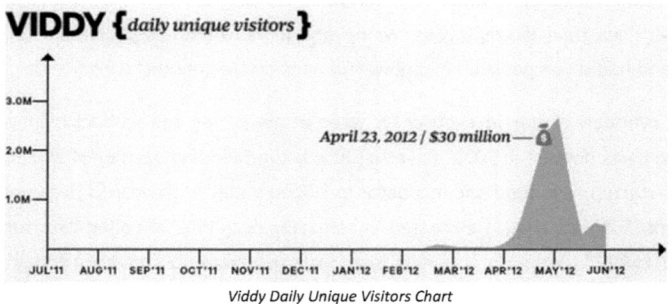

Viddy Daily Unique Visitors Chart

http://500.co/activate-or-die-3-keys-to-user-activation-for-saas-part-1

This graph is representative of what many SaaS startups experience. Improving your activation rate is an ongoing process that should be done along with other conversion rate optimisation efforts, such as '[breaking] down activation into steps, run A/B tests, focus on user drop-off areas' (Su, 2014). 'Viddy never nailed the activation piece. Many of the users that signed up never came back to the app again. Thus, when Facebook put a stop to their friend-blasting user acquisition approach, they went into a tailspin from which they haven't recovered' (Su, 2014).

It seems effective acquisition means nothing if you ignore the one key metric — activation. Activation is one of the most important metrics for any SaaS company. It's the second "A" in McClure's "AARRR", and 'it's a measure of the key action your users need to take to get value from your product, and how many users take that action' (Su, 2014).

Activation

As a partner at GrowHack, Conrad Wadowski works with venture backed companies and has this to say about activation:

> *Activation is the process of getting a new user to a must-have experience and a set of best practices to get them active. The best activation won't involve too much process. It mixes selling, education and using your product without too much friction.*
>
> *(Conrad Wadowski, 2013)*

He says that the best way to learn how to do this well is to learn from other products. After documenting over 70 activation flows from the best companies in the industry, some of the best tactics were leveraging motivation and testing ideas and talking to end users (Wadowski, 2013 - more in Appendix C).

Apart from reaching your target users, offering irresistible value, streamlining and simplifying on-boarding processes, there are decisions to be made as to what can be given away for free, which is a popular tactic for SaaS companies.

> *The activation problem only gets bigger when you venture beyond consumer products. 40-60% of users who sign up for a free trial of your software application will use it once and never come back again. Well, that sucks, but for better or worse, this is normal in SaaS.*
>
> *(Su, 2014)*

Retention

Quint (N/A) says that 'there are too many companies asking "How do we acquire more users?" that should instead be asking "How do we get better at keeping the users we already have?"'.

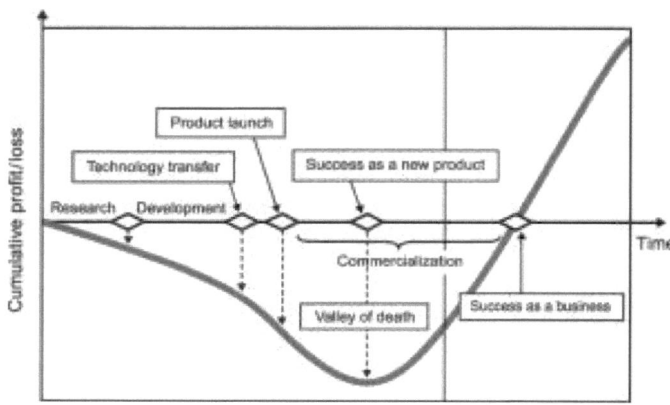

The Valley of Death

http://www.forbes.com/sites/martinzwilling/2013/02/18/10-ways-for-startups-to-survive-the-valley-of-death/

The "valley of death" is a common term in the startup world, referring to the difficulty of covering the negative cash flow in the early stages of a startup, before their new product or service is bringing in revenue from real customers (Zwilling, 2013). But getting to the product/market fit stage or 'out of the valley of death is the first thing that matters. Until then, bootstrap to buy yourself iterations and apply lean startup techniques to maximise learning from those iterations' (Maurya, 2010).

3 Stages of a Lean Startup

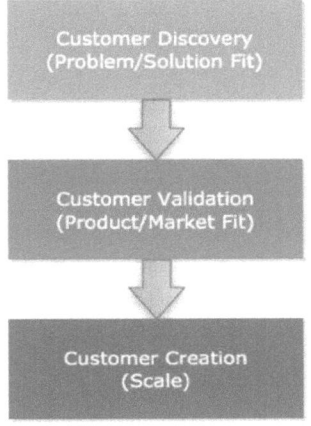

3 Stages of a Bootstrap

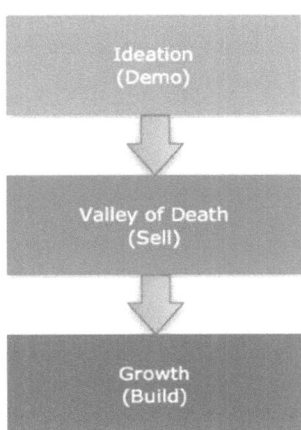

http://practicetrumpstheory.com/bootstrapping-a-lean-startup/

While not the same thing, Bootstrapping and Lean Startups are quite complementary. Both cover techniques for building low-burn startups by eliminating waste through the maximisation of existing resources first before expending effort on the acquisition of new or external resources. While bootstrapping provides a strategic roadmap for achieving sustainability through customer funding (i.e. charging customers), lean startups provide a more tactical approach to achieving those goals through validated learning.

(Maurya, 2010.)

Referral

Quint (N/A) warns businesses to 'not focus on improving virality unless your overall retention is stable, not continuing decrease after some reasonable period of time'.

Social networks are powerful drivers: 'Many services offer incentives for referring friends (which is more appealing when the product is free). And freemium is more successful than

30-day free trials or other limited-term offers, because customers have become wary of cumbersome cancellation processes and find indefinite free access more compelling' (Kumar, 2014). The monthly subscription fees typically charged are proving to be a more sustainable source of revenue than the advertising model prevalent among online firms in the early 2000s (Kumar, 2014).

Revenue

Several factors contribute to the appeal of a freemium strategy. 'Because free features are a potent marketing tool, the model allows a new venture to scale up and attract a user base without expending resources on costly ad campaigns or a traditional sales force' (Kumar, 2014). Despite its popularity and clear benefits, 'freemium is still poorly understood. It has inherent challenges, as demonstrated by the many start-ups that have tried but failed to make it work' (Kumar, 2014).

Springpad had difficulty monetising and 'considered offering notebooks for purchase, or generating income from affiliate conversions. They never rolled out a premium or freemium offering based on notebooks, choosing ad support over a freemium model, which required a lot more scale than they could ever achieve' (Ungerleider, 2014).

SECTION 4: RESEARCH METHOD

Technological innovations affecting web and app design will likely remain a powerful influence on businesses, requiring innovative cultures just to survive. The role of technology in economic growth spurs Philip Zelikow of the Markle Foundation to say that governments need to 'understand we are on the cusp of a transformation akin to the industrial revolution... [W]e adapted to those changes with things such as universal high school and electrification and we need the same kind of broad agenda now. We need to adapt again' (Miller, 2014). LinkedIn CEO Jeff Weiner observes that 'things were changing faster with the agrarian age developing over a millennium, the industrial age over a couple of centuries, and the information revolution over decades. But now in the digital economy, there is something new every day' (Miller, 2014).

While the tech industry celebrates successes—the startups which scale to Facebook or Amazon size, the startups which sell for huge dollar sums (even when, as is frequently the case, the startups generate products with no financial value or even a strategy to make a profit)—there's less attention paid to the companies which don't make it. Many times, the difference between a company's success or failure isn't the founders' savviness, the rockstar engineers, or the leadership's ability to get savvy advisors. Lots of times, it simply comes down to when a company enters the market (first is not always best) and—worst of all—bad luck.

(Ungerleider, 2014)

Fast changing times present fast changing problems which require faster changing solutions. Following the SaaS startups that scramble amidst their volatile markets is perhaps best left to the news aggregates such as Fast Company, Tech Crunch, 500.co, Business Insider, entrepreneur.com and Forbes, that keep abreast of the latest and current events.

SECTION 5: ANALYSIS

The increasing rate of emerging technologies causes organisations to 'place cardinal focus on factors that influence innovation and the success of innovation. Studies of organisations that have been consistently successful innovators indicate that they place great importance on managing and investing in the following components, which are their principal assets for innovation' (NSW HSC, N/A):

- **Information**; systems for obtaining reliable, current information about markets, technologies, research, etc in the area in which they operate.

- **Networks**; all organisations rely on networks of other organisations to make and supply materials, components, equipment, and often to provide services such as design, distribution, training, and advertising

- **Reputation**; innovations continue or fade away according to their reputation for style, quality, service, performance, status, etc.

- **Intellectual property**; developing and protecting their knowledge base through patents, design registrations, trademarks and copyright.

- **Funding**; innovation is risky and it usually requires considerable investment of time and money either from previous profits or from external funding, e.g. loans, grants, commissions, share issues, licences, royalties

These components should provide a much more detailed review to build upon the "AARRR" model applied to SaaS companies and how they have handled these factors.

Information; markets and technologies

If SaaS startups can find a niche market and differentiate themselves from their competitors, the reward can be great. Scott Knoll, CEO of Integral Ad Science (see Appendix D) says that '[t]he competition is fierce, because the barriers to entry are relatively low, and there is plenty of access to [venture capital] money' (Cutler, 2014). However, even if there is plenty of access to venture capital, it doesn't necessarily mean most startups actually have or utilise this access. What they do have is a product that they have worked hard on to attract users with the idea of monetising down the track. Knoll believes that '[s]o much opportunity exists for entrepreneurs because switching costs for most customers are low and many are willing to try new, relatively untested technologies' (Cutler, 2014).

Dropbox and LinkedIn are a study in contrasts (see Appendix E):

> The former has attracted 200 million users with a simple proposition: Everyone who enters a username and a password gets two gigabytes of cloud-based storage free. If people run out of space, they can pay $9.99 a month (or, alternatively, $99 a year) for 100 GB of storage. The free version is adequate for basic documents, but anyone who wants to back up photos or other media quickly hits the limit, and the reasons to upgrade are obvious.

> For many LinkedIn users, the advantages of upgrading are murkier... the ongoing value of doing so is not apparent. (The company offers four premium subscriptions, some aimed at specific customer segments, such as recruiters or salespeople, and most featuring deeper search functionality, better e-mail

capability, and more visibility into who has viewed your profile.) Although LinkedIn is successful—it was one of the first freemium companies to go public—it could probably monetise more users if the distinctions between its free and paid offerings were clearer.

(Kumar, 2014)

Networks/competition

In a recent editorial in The Wall Street Journal, Christopher Mims suggests that the wide-open web that launched a thousand new businesses and a million new ideas over the past two decades "is dying". In its place, he suggests, 'is the more proprietary, closed-off world of mobile apps' (McKendrick, 2014).

The web as it was designed, he says, 'created a commons where people could exchange information and goods. It forced companies to build technology designed to be compatible with competitors' technology. Emerging closed app ecosystems don't share those ideals of openness between vendors' offerings' (McKendrick, 2014).

This does not seem to stand up to the scrutiny of Tim Cadogan, CEO of OpenX, who urges that businesses should be 'looking for ways to enhance the products and services of other companies rather than compete with them... Find ways to complement existing products and companies so you don't take on unnecessary battles but embrace and extend everywhere and everyone except for your core area' (McKendrick, 2014).

Evernote is a shining example of playing well with others. In fact, not only do they embrace networking with other organisations, they commemorate it.

https://platformawards.evernote.com/vote/startups/

Evernote now has its own annual Platform Awards, celebrating the best apps that connect to Evernote (Evernote Corporation, 2015).

Evernote not only have many apps (see the 2014 award winners in Appendix F) that integrate with the software, they have entire collections.

https://appcenter.evernote.com/

Springpad had a more social approach, integrating with Google, Facebook and Twitter accounts. It behaved more like a personal assistant seamlessly running in the background; allowing reminders, using tags and finding comprehensive details of products by capturing barcodes, to name a few (Henry, 2012). Henry (2012) said '[o]ne of the most compelling things about Springpad is that [it was] growing and changing faster than most other services like it'. Compared to Evernote, Springpad may have dominated function, but it still had a lot of catching up to do in terms of acquiring users.

Reputation

In 2013, Springpad announced former Time VP Jacqueline Hampton would join the team as its new CEO. She said the company has 'built a strong product, one that people intuitively understand once she demonstrates it to them, but it needs to get its name out there' (Ha, 2013). Hampton emphasised the importance of building up awareness of the Springpad brand, pitching it as 'a unique mix between a private productivity app and a broader social search tool' (Ha, 2013).

Early on, a highly critical review of Evernote appeared by influential tech blogger Jason Kincaid. The review, titled "Evernote, the Bug-ridden Elephant", said 'Evernote's applications are glitchy to the extreme; they often feel as if they're held together by the engineering equivalent of duct tape... The apps are so laden with quirks that I've long held a deep-seated fear that perhaps some of my data has not been saved' (Agrawal, 2014).

These are not good thoughts to be associated with a service for which keeping important data "forever" is an important brand promise. One trait of a successful startup when faced with negative feedback or even PR crises is the ability to respond quickly and openly. The next day, Libin blogged that he 'could quibble with the specifics, but reading Jason's article was a painful and frustrating experience because, in the big picture, he's right. We're going to fix this' (Newton, 2014). He then proceeded to address the concerns and criticisms made by Kincaid in great depth and detail, with admiral transparency concerning the company.

Intellectual property

Because of such rapid changes in technology in the arenas of both hardware and software, perhaps the most important part of intellectual property a SaaS company should exert time and money for is design. Design, both functional and aesthetic, is the face of a company that greets its users — what they interact with. A bad design experience can be a huge contributing factor to poor customer acquisition, which preludes activation.

http://appadvice.com/appnn/2010/03/organize-your-entire-life-with-springpad

The Springpad app was designed as an organiser for recipes, movies to watch, home improvement projects, and interior design projects. Essentially, it did everything Pinterest did—but two years before Pinterest entered the market. Crucially, their core product was designed for clipping items for later purchase (Ungerleider, 2014). Henry (2012) thought that Springpad was 'a more elegant and visually attractive way of organising your life than Evernote, and a more useful way of organising the things you find on the web than Pinterest'.

Libin said that Evernote strived to 'have a culture of design, so we need to make a culture in the company that basically says that design is the most important thing and evaluating constant improvement in design is the central element to what we do, but to have that culture we need to design it. We have this feedback loop where we're trying to design a culture of design' (Baer, 2013).

Evernote's icon is clearly superior, touting an elephant—a well-known symbol for memory—with a peeling document for an ear. (Appendix G contains a video that shows an in-depth behind-the-scenes run-down of the branding creative process.) This may be evidence of their successes in raising capital and having it at their disposal.

Funding

Kumar (2014) asserts that 'one of the chief purposes of freemium is to attract new users. If you're not succeeding with that goal, it probably means that your free offerings are not compelling enough and you need to provide more or better features free. If you're generating lots of traffic but few people are paying to upgrade, you may have the opposite problem: Your free offerings are too rich, and it's time to cut back'(Kumar, 2014).

Although Springpad's product anticipated market needs, their 2008 launch date occurred before the mobile app economy fully bloomed. Even worse, they did not know how to make money off of their free service. Cofounder Jeff Janer said: 'We built a heck of a product... but we didn't build the business. In that respect, given our background, we wanted to provide useful information to people that could be monetised' (Ungerleider, 2014).

When Springpad announced they had run out of money in May 2014, 'their large user community was blindsided. Springpad had built a niche for themselves as an organising product that had more functionality than Pinterest but was much easier to use then Evernote; and yet, by the time they realised they had missed the monetisation boat, it was too late' (Ungerleider, 2014).

SECTION 6: SYNTHESIS

Once considered an Evernote rival, Springpad 'failed to develop a monetisation strategy—and despite their best efforts (and rumoured acquisitions by Amazon and Google), things just didn't turn around in time. On June 25, Springpad closed its doors' (Ungerleider, 2014).

Evernote's CEO Phil Libin philosophises:

> [T]here comes a time in a booming startup's life when it's important to pause for a bit and look in rather than up. When it's more important to improve existing features than to add new ones. More important to make our existing users happier than to just add more new users. More important to focus on our direction than on our speed. This is just common sense, but startups breathe growth and intentionally slowing down to focus on details and quality doesn't come naturally to many of us. Despite this, the best product companies in the world have figured out how to make constant quality improvements part of their essential DNA. Apple and Google and Amazon and Facebook and Twitter and Tesla know how to do this. So will we.
>
> (Libin, 2014)

Jeremy Roberts, the author of Evernote Every Day: Getting More Out of Evernote, wonders 'if perhaps when the Springpad team went to seek capital to expand the business into a model that encompassed professional use, investors failed to see the value that Springpad could provide to the business world. It's sad because I'm sure that Springpad would have been really great for many organisations, such as design agencies' (Ungerleider, 2014).

SECTION 7: RESEARCH RESULTS

Contributing factors to SaaS survival and the major areas of the various SaaS business models can mostly be summarised by some of the experts in their fields.

Information/Intellectual Property

Design and technology are symbiotic when it comes to internet software and applications. Springpad may have won the battle for best use of technology and usability, but Evernote's branding came out on top, which along with marketing efforts was perhaps one of the driving factors for their vastly superior user acquisition.

Acquisition/Reputation

A very high conversion rate isn't necessarily good, as one of the benefits of a freemium model is the ability to acquire users and generate traffic.

> *You would do better to convert 5% of 2 million monthly visitors, for example, than to convert 50% of 100,000 visitors. The best long-term strategy is generally to aim for a moderate conversion rate (in my research, I've found that most companies' range from 2% to 5%) coupled with a high volume of traffic. If you're targeting a small market, you should aim for a higher rate.*
>
> *(Kumar, 2014)*

Maintaining a transparent image is instrumental in keeping a helpful and responsive reputation. Fostering user relationships and focusing on keeping them engaged and happy may at times be more valuable in keeping them onboard, rather than continuously expanding product functionality.

Activation

Offering a product with overly broad functionality can be a great incentive for activating users, although the larger the functionality, the greater the maintenance. This may become too much of an endeavour for small startups with limited resources. By welcoming interaction with other similar or complimentary services, a startup can concern themselves with the value of their smaller product, while maintaining an ongoing presence.

Referral/Networks

As with Viddy's experience using social media to rapidly expand a user-base, if there is not enough lasting value, subscriptions will quickly subside.

> If you're thinking in 100-year terms, the culture is the only important thing. The culture is everything in the long-term. The culture is much more important than the current product. The product is the current product, the culture is the next hundred products. This is what's going to produce everything.

> (Baer, 2013)

Retention

Knoll says that despite the success of a startup, 'there will always be new companies who will try to do what you do better and cheaper' (Cutler, 2014). Startups will always face tough competition, no matter how big they become. So while branding seems to be set in stone and it's assured that the product will change with the times, what is left is the problem of not only acquiring users, but also keeping them. This also points back to the importance of a strong culture.

Funding/Revenue

Zwilling (2013) finds that in reality, 'the financing valley of death tests the commitment, determination, and problem solving ability of every entrepreneur. It's the time when you create tremendous value out of nothing'.

The good news is that the cost for new startups is at an all-time low. In the early days (20 years ago), most new e-commerce sites cost a million dollars to set up. Now the price is closer to $100, if you are willing to do the work yourself. Software apps that once required a 10-person team can now be done with the Lean Development methodology by two people in a couple of months.

(Zwilling, 2013)

The freemium model seems to still be an ongoing experiment for many SaaS companies. When small percentages of user bases are activated, some have success through sheer numbers, while others do not know how to make money off of their free service. This comes down to how startups tackle the problem of adapting and remaining relevant in today's ephemeral market.

SECTION 8: CONCLUSION

SaaS startups need to stay focused on global changes, with particular attention on both the promise and perils facing the world and technology. The view of the internet is changing from models focused around advertising to those focused around commerce. Patrick Collison of Stripe believes that '[w]hat once made money largely by "collecting subsidies for entertainment" is now increasingly becoming a utility offering "magic wands for the world"' (Miller, 2014).

If customers don't clearly grasp what they would gain by upgrading within the popular freemium model, businesses may monetise fewer of them than they might otherwise expect. SaaS startups should continually prepare and account for competition and watch out for industry changes. But the question remains — what is the transition where at some point a business is no longer a startup?

Evernote wanted to 'make something that would be long-term, that was going to be sustainable, but it wasn't enough to just make a 100-year-old company. Just because they've been around for a long time doesn't necessarily make them great places to be' (Baer, 2013).

CEO Libin shares his vision at Dublin's 2013 Web Summit:

"It's impossible to know what the product will be in 100 years but it's easy to know what the brand will be... We want Evernote to be the most visible brand for people who care about productivity, being smart, and their minds." (Shontell, 2013)

Katin Miller, Springpad's head of user engagement said they 'ran out of money, that's basically the end of the story. It was a timing problem' (Ungerleider, 2014).

During the video, Top Tips for New Creative Business (found in Appendix A), Managing Director of Portable Content, Simon Goodrich expertly offers an outstanding overview and advice for startups:

"Try and be different. There's a lot of web developers out there. Experience counts, so if you think you're good, build your own app, build your own product, it's yours and you own it. Don't get too tied down into IP at the outset. Just do. From a product point of view, set expectations. Don't necessarily go too early if you're not ready. From a service point of view- same thing again-you don't launch until you're ready. The thing with websites, everyone can see them. If there's a fault, people know about it pretty quickly. People talk about it pretty quickly through social media. Also, just set your expectations. You're not going to take the world over overnight. You're not going to be the world's biggest application. Look, you may be. There's definitely Googles out there, but the reason we know about them is because there are so few of them. Just because you hear stories about people acquiring companies for multitudes of millions of dollars, it doesn't happen every day. It's not going to happen to you and don't think it's going to happen to you because if you do, it will really cloud your judgement and you'll make terribly poor decisions on how you're going to grow a business. At the end of the day, running a business within the digital media space is no different from running a business a hundred years ago. Become profitable, manage your expectations, make sure your income is more than your expenses and grow as you can grow."

(Creative Innovation, 2014)

SECTION 9: BIBLIOGRAPHY

500hats (N/A) About Dave McClure, Available at:
http://500hats.typepad.com/500blogs/about-dave-mcclure.html (Accessed: 10th January 2015).

Agrawal, Rakesh (2014) Evernote's Phil Libin shows how to do startup PR the right way, Available at: http://venturebeat.com/2014/01/08/evernotes-phil-libin-shows-how-to-do-startup-pr-the-right-way (Accessed: 7th January 2015).

Baer, Drake (2013) Evernote's Quest to Become a 100-Year-Old Startup, Available at: http://www.fastcompany.com/3012870/dialed/evernotes-quest-to-become-a-100-year-old-startup (Accessed: 6th January 2015).

Creative Innovation (2014) Creative Industries Innovation Centre, Available at: http://vimeo.com/cinnovation (Accessed: 7th January 2015).

Creative Innovation (2010) Top Tips for New Creative Business — Extended Version, Available at: http://vimeo.com/15420271 (Accessed: 6th January 2015).

Cutler, Zach (2014) 4 Big Challenges That Startups FACE, Available at: http://www.entrepreneur.com/article/240742 (Accessed: 10th January 2015).

Cutmull, Edwin (2014) Creativity, Inc.: Overcoming the Unseen Forces That Stand in the Way of True Inspiration, Canada: Random House.

Empson, Rip (2012) Attn. Evernote & Pinterest: Springpad's New Social Experience Turns Interests Into Action, Available at: http://techcrunch.com/2012/04/11/springpad-three-point-oh (Accessed: 5th January 2015).

Evernote Corporation (2015) Evernote Platform Awards, Available at: https://platformawards.evernote.com/vote/startups (Accessed: 10th January 2015).

Fell, Jason (2014) Under the Radar: 10 Startups to Watch in 2014, Available at: http://www.entrepreneur.com/slideshow/231561 (Accessed: 6th January 2015).

Ford, Rory (2012) AARRR Focus Me Hearties, Available at: http://pollenizer.com/aarrr-focus-me-hearties (Accessed: 9th January 2015).

Gompers, Paul & Lerner, Josh (2001) The Money of Invention: How Venture Capital Creates New Wealth, Boston: Harvard Business School Press.

Ha, Anthony (2013) Former Time VP Jacqueline Hampton Joins Springpad As Its New CEO, Available at: http://techcrunch.com/2013/08/13/jacqueline-hampton-joins-springpad (Accessed: 9th January 2015).

Henry, Alan (2012) How To Use Springpad As Your New Personal Assistant, Available at: http://www.lifehacker.com.au/2012/04/how-to-use-springpad-as-your-new-personal-assistant (Accessed: 10th January 2015).

Kumar, Vineet (2014) Making "Freemium" Work, Available at: https://hbr.org/2014/05/making-freemium-work (Accessed: 6th January 2015).

Libin, Phil (2014) On Software Quality and Building a Better Evernote in 2014, Available at: http://blog.evernote.com/blog/2014/01/04/on-software-quality/?fb_action_ids=10101102485756568&fb_action_types=og.likes (Accessed: 10th January 2015).

Maurya, Ash (2010) Bootstrapping a Lean Startup, Available at: http://practicetrumpstheory.com/bootstrapping-a-lean-startup (Accessed: 6th January 2015).

McClure, Dave (2007) Product Marketing for Pirates: AARRR! (aka Startup Metrics for Internet Marketing & Product Management), Available at: http://500hats.typepad.com/500blogs/2007/06/internet-market.html (Accessed: 6th January 2015).

McKendrick, Joe (2014) Are mobile apps destroying the openness of the web? Available at: http://www.zdnet.com/article/are-mobile-apps-destroying-the-openness-of-the-web (Accessed: 6th January 2015).

Miller, Michael (2014) Techonomy looks at the future of man and machines, Available at: http://au.pcmag.com/csiro/26243/opinion/techonomy-looks-at-the-future-of-man-and-machines (Accessed: 7th January 2015).

Mullin, Shanelle (2013) The Beginner's Guide to Startup Analytics, Available at: https://blog.kissmetrics.com/startup-analytics (Accessed: 9th January 2015).

Newton, Casey (2014) Evernote CEO acknowledges stability issues, says simpler design is coming, Available at: http://www.theverge.com/2014/1/5/5276654/evernote-ceo-acknowledges-stability-issues-says-simpler-design-is (Accessed: 10th January 2015).

NSW HSC (N/A) Innovation and emerging technologies, Available at: http://hsc.csu.edu.au/design_technology/innovation_emerging/factors/success_failure/1.2.11.html (Accessed: 8th January 2015).

Pirate Metrics (2015) Actionable analytics, Available at: http://piratemetrics.com (Accessed: 8th January 2015).

Quint, Jamie (N/A) Retention is King, Available at: http://andrewchen.co/retention-is-king (Accessed: 8th January 2015).

Rao, Leena (2011) Evernote Rival SpringPad Springs Past 1 Million Users, Available at: http://techcrunch.com/2011/02/11/evernote-rival-springpad-springs-past-1-million-users (Accessed: 9th January 2015).

Shontell, Alyson (2013) How Evernote's Phil Libin Plans To Build A '100-Year Startup', Available at: http://www.businessinsider.com.au/how-evernotes-phil-libin-plans-to-build-a-100-year-startup-2013-10 (Accessed: 6th January 2015).

Su, Susan (2014) Activate or Die: 3 Keys to User Activation for SaaS (Part 1), Available at: http://500.co/activate-or-die-3-keys-to-user-activation-for-saas-part-1 (Accessed: 7th January 2015).

Ungerleider, Neal (2014) This Startup Had Over 5 Million Users and a Great Product. Then it Folded: The (Somewhat) Surprising Demise of the Popular Organising App Springpad—And What Happened Next. Available at: http://www.fastcompany.com/3032341/most-creative-people/this-startup-had-over-5-million-users-and-a-great-product-then-it-folde (Accessed: 8th January 2015).

Vidra, Eze (2014) Startup Resources (Updated August 2014), Available at: http://www.vccafe.com/startup-resources (Accessed: 9th January 2015).

Wadowski, Conrad (2013) Growth Hacking: Acquire New Users with Better Activation, Available at: http://www.slideshare.net/conradwadowski/growth-hacking-user-onboarding (Accessed: 9th January 2015).

Zwilling, Martin (2013) 10 Ways For Startups To Survive The Valley Of Death, Available at: http://www.forbes.com/sites/martinzwilling/2013/02/18/10-ways-for-startups-to-survive-the-valley-of-death (Accessed: 6th January 2015).

SECTION 10: APPENDICES

Appendix A

The Creative Industries Innovation Centre is dedicated to growing the potential of Australia's creative enterprises, big and small (Creativeinnovation, 2014).

Ctrl+click to watch their video: Top Tips for New Creative Business.

http://vimeo.com/15420271

Appendix B

Web Strategy for Pirates (AARRR).

Customer Lifecycle / Conversion Behavior

- **A**cquisition: users from misc channels come to site
  - or landing page, or widget, etc
- **A**ctivation: users enjoy 1st site visit, "happy" user experience
  - view X pages, spend Y seconds, make Z clicks
- **R**etention: users re-visit site multiple times
  - ex: 3+ visits in first 30 days
  - type: cookied user, email / account, content / RSS, etc
- **R**eferral: users like product enough to refer others
  - referral happens via email, links, blogs, widgets, word-of-mouth, etc
- **R**evenue: users conduct monetization behavior
  - if no monetization, choose next-best proxy (free download, etc)

Customer Lifecycle / Conversion Behavior

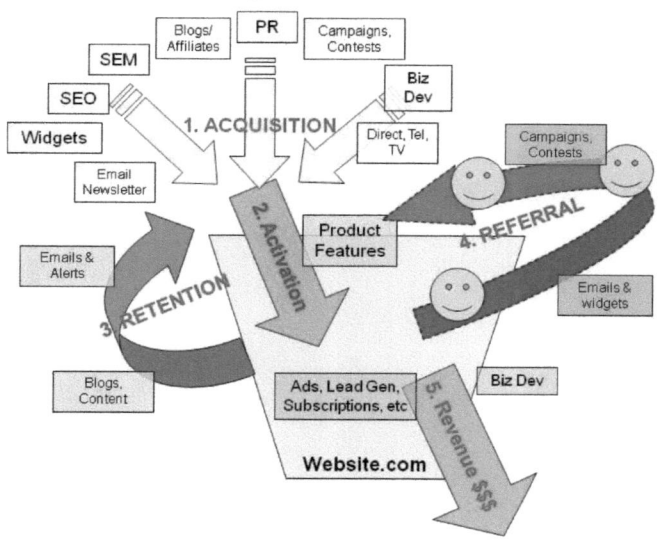

Example Conversion Metrics

*(note: *not* actuals; your mileage may vary...)*

Category	User Status	Conv %	Est. Value
Acquisition	**Visit Site** (or landing page, or external widget)	100%	$.01
Acquisition	**Doesn't Abandon** (views 2+ pages, stays 10+ sec, 2+ clicks)	70%	$.05
Activation	**Happy 1ˢᵗ Visit** (views X pages, stays Y sec, Z clicks)	30%	$.25
Activation	**Email/Blog/RSS/Widget Signup** (anything that could lead to repeat visit)	5%	$1
Activation	**Acct Signup** (includes profile data)	2%	$3
Retention	**Email Open / RSS view -> Clickthru**	3%	$2
Retention	**Repeat Visitor** (3+ visits in first 30 days)	2%	$5
Referral	**Refer 1+ users who visit site**	2%	$3
Referral	**Refer 1+ users who activate**	1%	$10
Revenue	**User generates minimum revenue**	2%	$5
Revenue	**User generates break-even revenue**	1%	$25

http://www.slideshare.net/dmc500hats/startup-metrics-for-pirates-long-version

There is even an analytics SaaS based on this strategy called Pirate Metrics, which helps perform quantitative and comparative analysis of businesses by tracking the 5 key metrics (Pirate Metrics, 2015).

Appendix C

Growth Hacking: Acquire New Users with Better Activation.

(Ctrl+click to follow link)

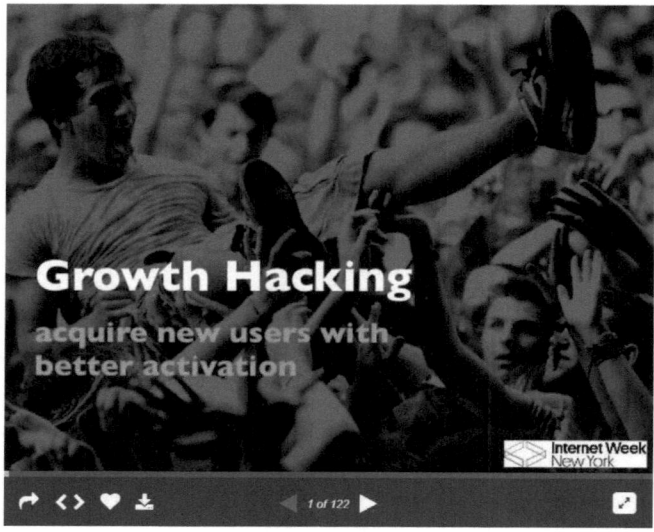

http://www.slideshare.net/conradwadowski/growth-hacking-user-onboarding

Appendix D

Integral Ad Science is a leading ad-tech company that assesses and reports value of each ad opportunity to help media buyers and sellers maximise return on investment.

Appendix E

A graph comparing Dropbox and Linkedin's freemium differences:

	Dropbox	LinkedIn	NYTimes.com	Spotify
WHAT IT IS	A cloud storage and file-sharing service	A social media site for professional networking	A digital, enhanced version of the print newspaper	A music streaming and downloading service
WHAT'S FREE	2 GB of storage, with up to 16 GB more for referring friends	Creating a profile, making connections, basic communication	10 articles a month	Unlimited music, interspersed with ads
WHAT'S PREMIUM	100 GB of storage for $9.99 a month	Advanced searches and communication, starting at $19.95 a month	Full access, starting at $3.75 a week	Downloads and ad-free streaming for $9.99 a month
HOW MANY USE IT	More than 200 million users (free and premium)	277 million users (free and premium) at the end of 2013	53.8 million visitors in December 2013; 760,000 subscribers	24 million users, of whom 6 million are subscribers

https://hbr.org/2014/05/making-freemium-work/ar/1

Appendix F

The 2014 winners of the Evernote Platform Awards:

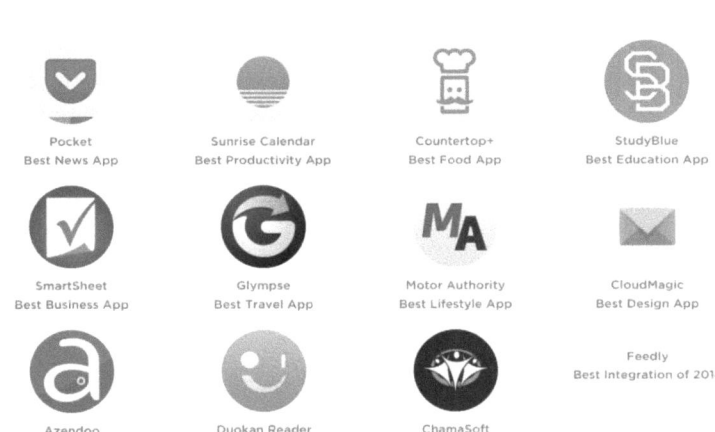

Pocket Best News App	Sunrise Calendar Best Productivity App	Countertop+ Best Food App	StudyBlue Best Education App
SmartSheet Best Business App	Glympse Best Travel App	Motor Authority Best Lifestyle App	CloudMagic Best Design App
Azendoo Best Multi-Platform App	Duokan Reader Best Yingxiang Biji App	ChamaSoft Africa Innovation Award	Feedly Best Integration of 2014

https://platformawards.evernote.com/vote/startups/

Appendix G

"Icon to Interface – Evernote Trunk Conference" covers the initial scope of logo ideas, in-depth reasoning, logical and practical considerations of implementing the Evernote logo/icon across the entire brand identity.

(Ctrl+click to follow link)

http://youtu.be/f9_EYK1BHrg